In My Backyard

Written by
Nancy Bizarria-Ramos

Art by
TullipStudio

Copyright ©2021 by Nancy Bizarria-Ramos

All rights reserved. No part of this book may be reproduced in any form on by an electronic or mechanical means, including information storage and retrieval systems, without permission in writing from the author, except by a reviewer who may quote brief passages in a review.

Dedicated to my two children who continue to inspire me every day.

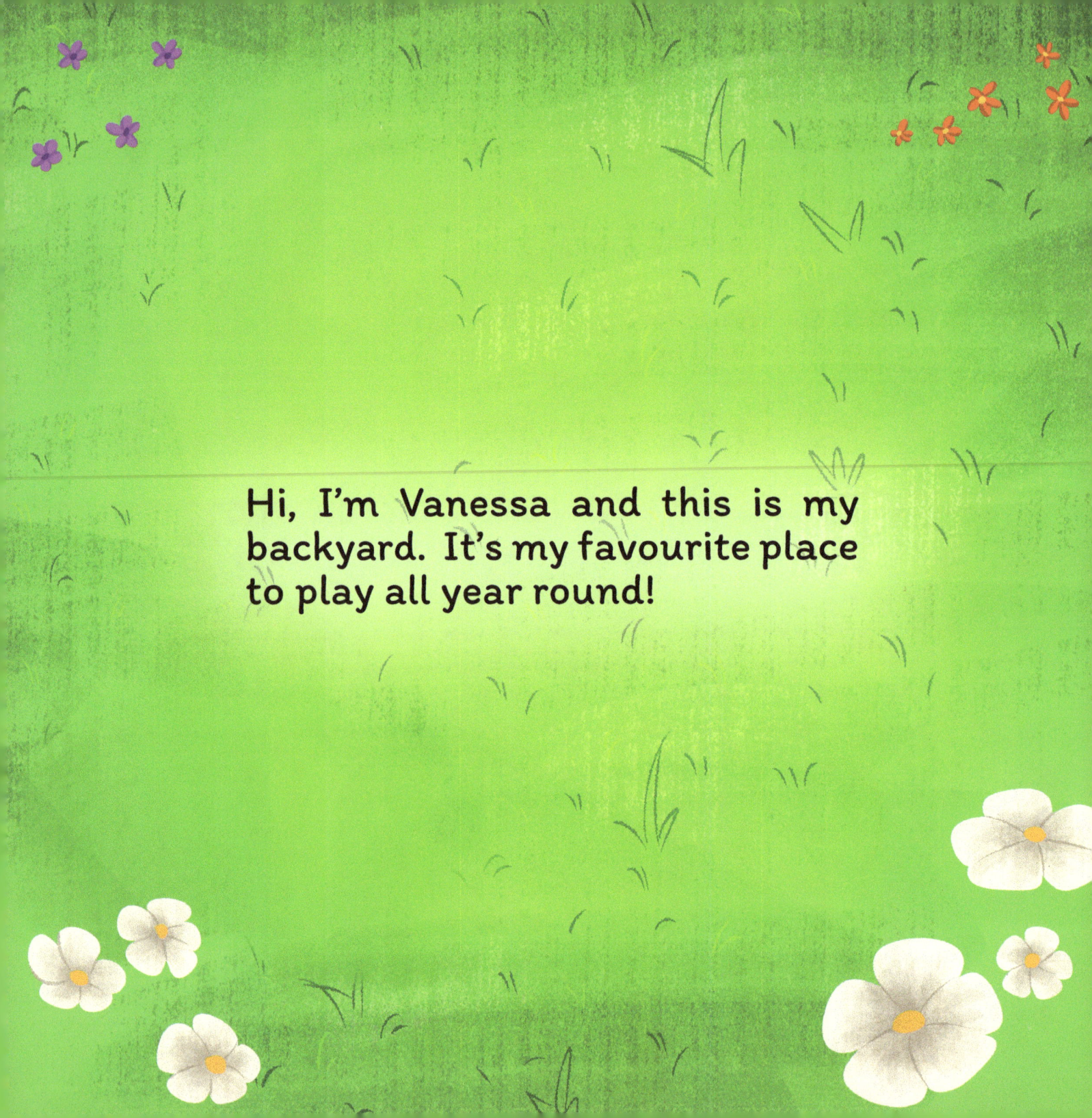

Hi, I'm Vanessa and this is my backyard. It's my favourite place to play all year round!

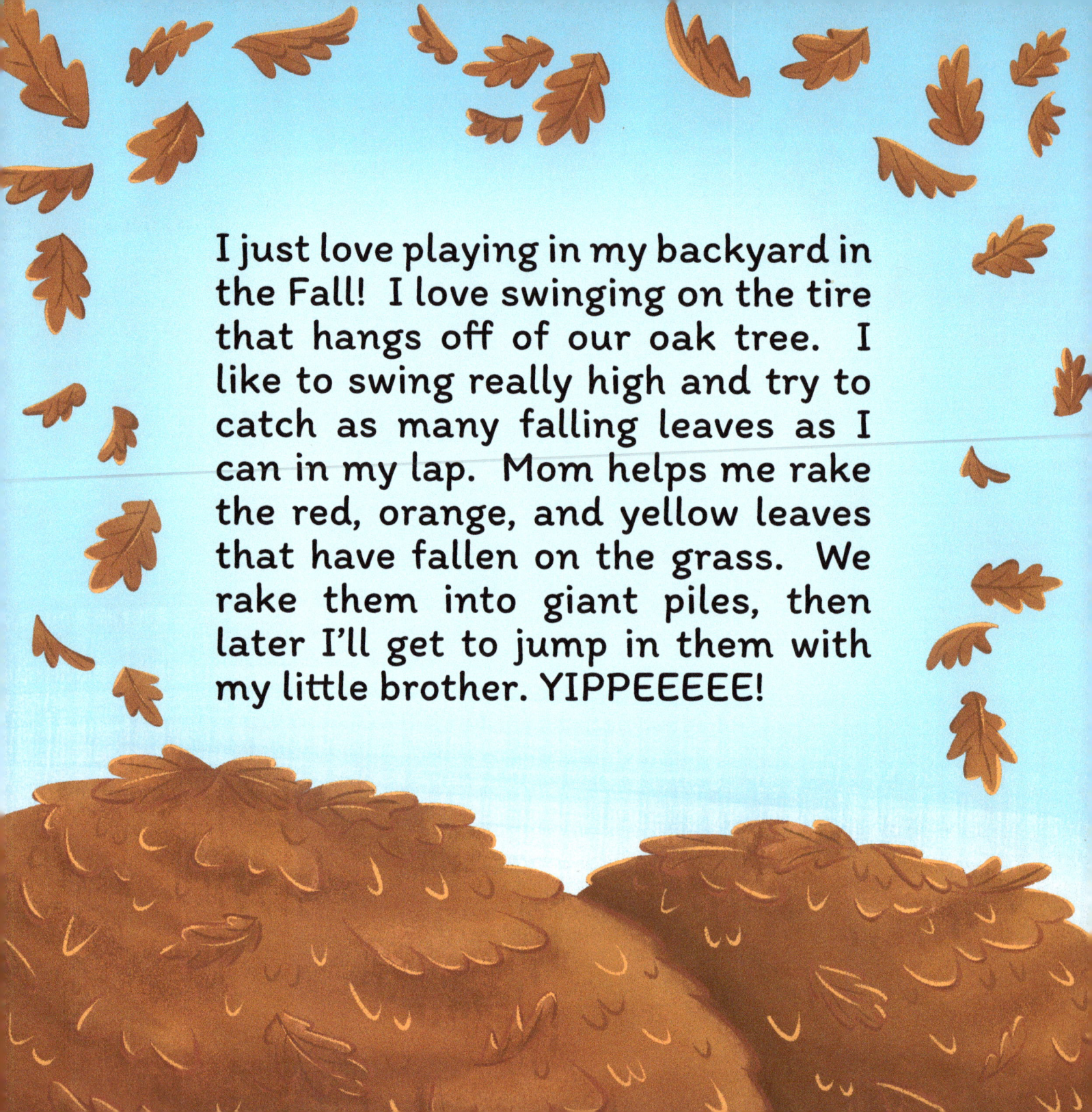

I just love playing in my backyard in the Fall! I love swinging on the tire that hangs off of our oak tree. I like to swing really high and try to catch as many falling leaves as I can in my lap. Mom helps me rake the red, orange, and yellow leaves that have fallen on the grass. We rake them into giant piles, then later I'll get to jump in them with my little brother. YIPPEEEEE!

It starts to get a little colder now, so I have to wear my big fluffy red sweater that grandma knitted me. Pretty soon it will get dark, and mom will be calling me to come inside for dinner. That's ok, I'm starting to get a little hungry now anyway.

During Wintertime I love to run out and stomp around, listening to the snow crunch beneath my favourite pair of pink winter boots.

I let myself fall backwards into the soft fluffy snow. It feels like I'm laying in a giant bowl of flour! Fluffy snow is great for making snow angels.

I love rolling snow around the ground and making 1....2....3 snowballs, just enough to make a snowgirl.

I have two black buttons for her eyes, a baby carrot for her nose, a handful of raisins for her smile, and one of grandma's old sun hats for her head.

There...now she looks perfect!

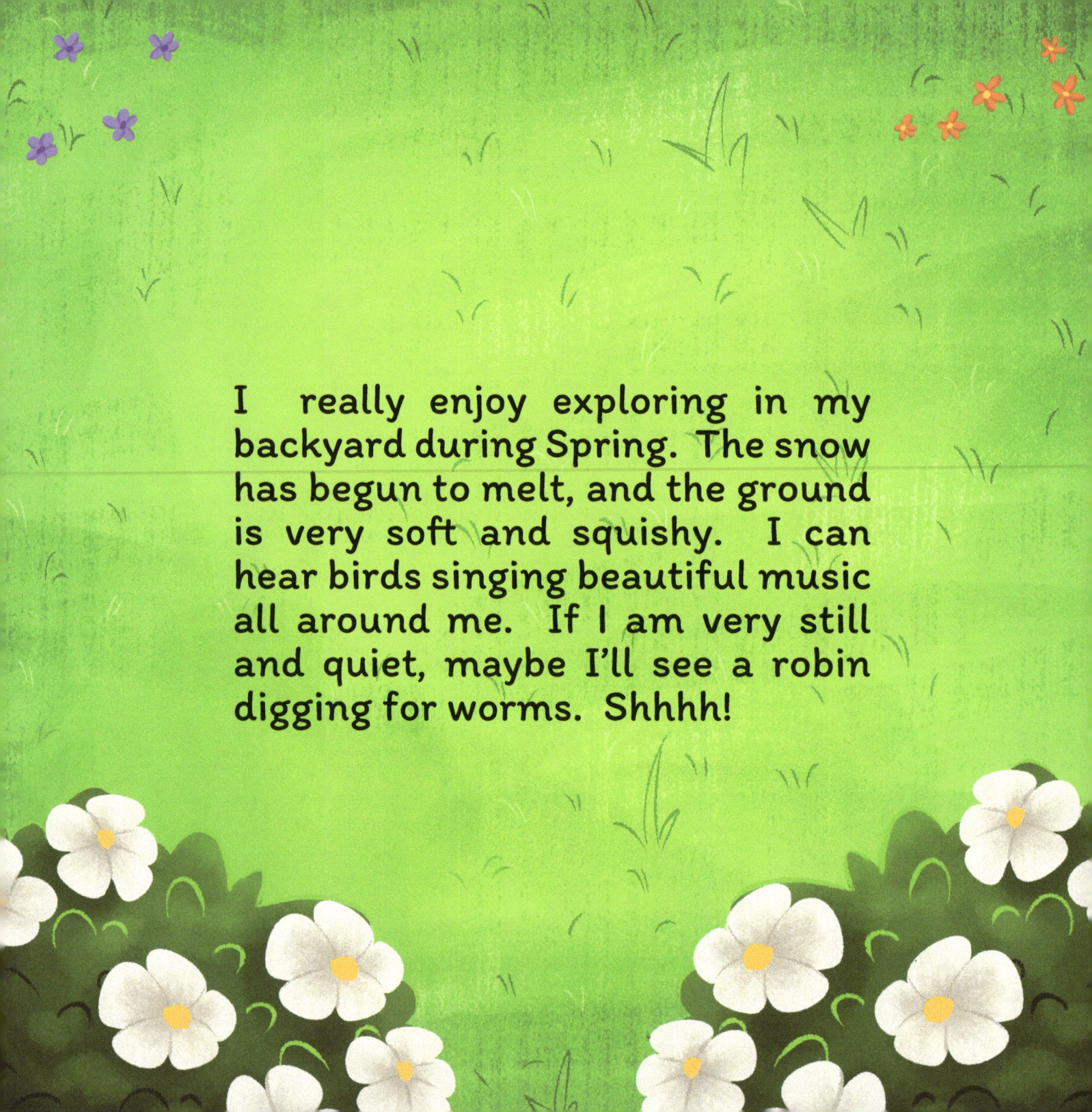

I really enjoy exploring in my backyard during Spring. The snow has begun to melt, and the ground is very soft and squishy. I can hear birds singing beautiful music all around me. If I am very still and quiet, maybe I'll see a robin digging for worms. Shhhh!

The buds on the apple tree are just starting to open up and play peek-a-boo with me. I helped dad plant pink and purple tulips in our garden last fall, and now they are starting to bloom. I get to water them with my new blue watering can!

Sometimes when it rains, I get to dress up in my raincoat and my yellow rubber boots, and jump around the puddles in my backyard! My mom says that she can't wait till summertime when it doesn't rain as much, and my clothes don't get so dirty!

Finally, Summertime arrives in my backyard! It's my favourite season. Mom bought me a new pink bathing suit. It has a big red flower on the front of it. I think it's just beautiful. I can't wait till dad fills up our pool with the water hose.

When it's ready, SPLASH!!! In the pool I jump. What fun! I love to float on my back and stare up at the clouds in the sky. Ooooh, I can see one shaped like a cat. Look over there! There is one shaped like an ice cream cone. Yummy!

By now we have a whole bunch of pretty flowers growing in my backyard. My favourite ones are the white daisies and the purple pansies. WOW! Look over there by the bright orange milkweeds. It's a Monarch butterfly! Isn't she lovely? Maybe I can get a closer look if I move very slowly.

Mom says it's time to come inside now. It's starting to get dark, and soon there will be hungry mosquitoes flying around everywhere. That's all right, I guess. There will be lots of time tomorrow to play again, in my backyard.

The End

About the Author

Nancy Bizarria-Ramos was born and raised in Brampton, Ontario, Canada. Proud mother of two children, Vanessa and Thomas. She obtained her diploma in Early Childhood Education, and has since then worked with children of various special needs, in the school setting for over 20 years.

BIZARRIA_RAMOS

www.ingramcontent.com/pod-product-compliance
Lightning Source LLC
Chambersburg PA
CBHW061121170426
43209CB00013B/1629